NATIONAL GEOGRAPHIC

Tornadoes

EXTREME WEATHER

Josie Green

PICTURE CREDITS
Cover: © Getty Images

page 4 (bottom left) Despotovic Dusko/Corbis Sygma; page 5 (top), page 9 (top), page 11, 12 © Getty Images; page 15 © Corbis; page 16 © AFP/Corbis; page 22 (top), page 25, National Oceanic and Atmospheric Admistration/Department of Commerce; page 23 © AP/Fotopress; page 26 © AFP/Corbis.

Produced through the worldwide resources of the National Geographic Society, John M. Fahey, Jr., President and Chief Executive Officer; Gilbert M. Grosvenor, Chairman of the Board; Nina D. Hoffman, Executive Vice President and President, Books and Education Publishing Group.

PREPARED BY NATIONAL GEOGRAPHIC SCHOOL PUBLISHING
Ericka Markman, Senior Vice President and President, Children's Books and Education Publishing Group; Steve Mico, Vice President and Editorial Director; Marianne Hiland, Executive Editor; Richard Easby, Editorial Manager; Jim Hiscott, Design Manager; Kristin Hanneman, Illustrations Manager; Matt Wascavage, Manager of Publishing Services; Sean Philpotts, Production Manager.

EDITORIAL MANAGEMENT
Morrison BookWorks, LLC

PROGRAM CONSULTANTS
Dr. Shirley V. Dickson, Program Director, Literacy, Education Commission of the States; James A. Shymansky, E. Desmond Lee Professor of Science Education, University of Missouri-St. Louis.

National Geographic Theme Sets program developed by Macmillan Science and Education Australia Pty Limited.

Published by the National Geographic Society
1145 17th Street, N.W.
Washington, D.C. 20036-4688

ISBN: 978-0-7922-4724-1
ISBN: 0-7922-4724-8

Product 41964

Printed in China by The Central Printing (Hong Kong) Ltd.
Quarry Bay, Hong Kong
Supplier Code: OCP May 2018
Macmillan Job: 804263
Cengage US PO: 15308030

MEA10_May18_S

Contents

Extreme Weather. 4

Weather and Tornadoes. 6

Think About the Key Concepts. 17

Visual Literacy
Weather Maps. 18

Genre Study
Explanations. 20

Oklahoma Tornadoes, May 3, 1999. 21

Apply the Key Concepts. 27

Research and Write
Create Your Own Explanation. 28

Glossary. 31

Index. 32

Extreme Weather

The weather affects people's lives in many different ways. Weather helps people decide what clothes to wear, or what to do in their spare time. However, the weather can also be a matter of life and death. Extreme weather can be very severe. Droughts, floods, tornadoes, and hurricanes are all examples of extreme weather.

Key Concepts

1. **Conditions in the atmosphere, such as air pressure, create weather.**
2. **Clouds give meteorologists clues about what is happening in the atmosphere.**
3. **Tools and technology help meteorologists gather data about weather.**

Four Kinds of Extreme Weather

Droughts

Droughts happen when there is a lack of rain.

Floods

Floods happen when too much water flows over the land.

In this book you will learn about the causes and effects of tornadoes like this one.

Tornadoes

Tornadoes are spinning wind funnels that create strong suction.

Hurricanes

Hurricanes are powerful storms with strong winds and heavy rains.

Weather and Tornadoes

Imagine looking out the window and seeing a fierce twisting funnel reaching down from dark thunderclouds. This funnel is a tornado. It speeds across the landscape, ripping apart everything in its path. It pulls trees out at their roots. It tears buildings to shreds. It sucks animals into the sky. In minutes, the tornado has gone. All is quiet. But this violent storm has left a trail of destruction.

A Powerful Twister

Tornadoes are often called "twisters." The name refers to their shape and what they do. A tornado is made up of quickly spinning winds that form the shape of a funnel. Tornadoes have the strongest winds on Earth. They are the most violent of all storms.

Tornadoes are created in thunderstorms. Their strong winds twist down to reach land. They act like giant vacuum cleaners, sucking up objects in their way, such as trees, buildings, and cars. Then, when the tornado's force fades, the objects are dropped back to Earth.

Tornadoes often last only a few minutes. But they can cause millions of dollars of damage to buildings and roads. They can injure and kill people. Many other people can be left homeless. It can take a town or city a long time to recover from a tornado.

Tornadoes happen in many parts of the world. But the United States has the most tornadoes. They usually occur in an area known as "Tornado Alley." This area is in the middle of the United States, east of the Rocky Mountains and west of the Appalachian Mountains.

Tornadoes can cause a lot of damage.

Places Where Tornadoes Can Occur

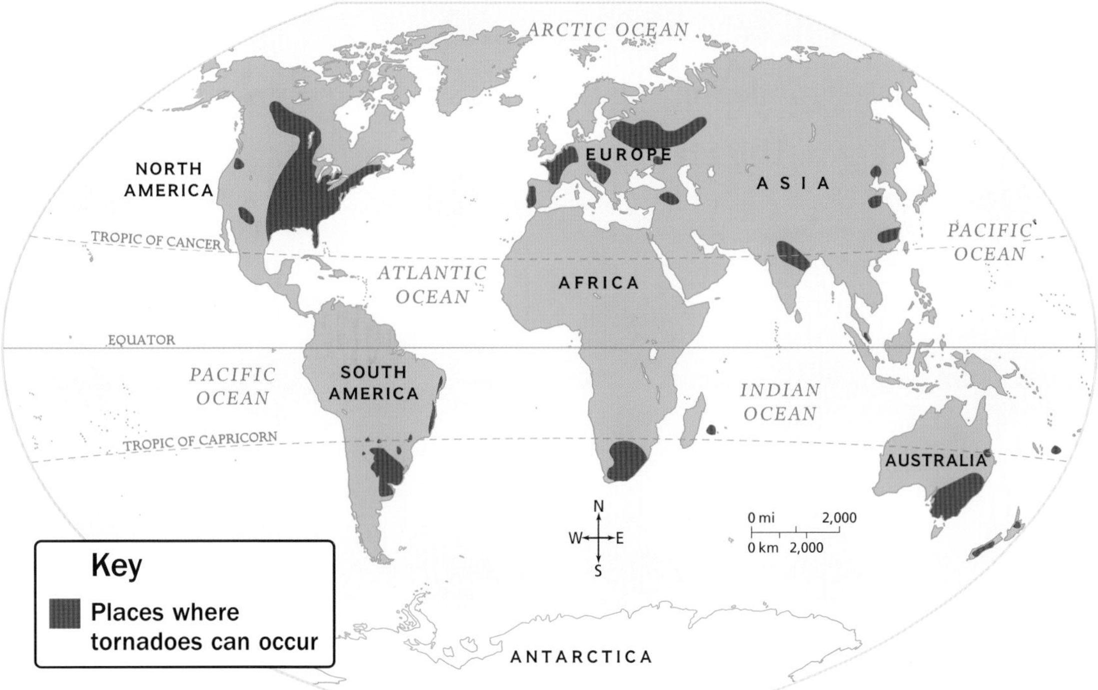

Key Concept 1 **Conditions in the atmosphere, such as air pressure, create weather.**

Where Wind Comes From

To understand what causes a tornado, you first have to understand where wind comes from. Wind is created by changes in air pressure and temperature. Earth is surrounded by a layer of air called the **atmosphere**. This layer of air presses down on Earth's surface. This is called **air pressure**.

atmosphere
the layer of air that surrounds Earth

air pressure
the effect of air pressing down on Earth's surface

The air does not always push down on Earth with the same amount of force. When air is warmed by the sun, it becomes lighter and rises into the sky. When this warm air rises, there is less air pushing down on that area of Earth. This creates an area of **low air pressure**.

When air is high up it cools, and its **particles** move closer together. This makes the air heavy, or **dense**. The heavy air sinks and presses down more on Earth in that area. This creates an area of **high air pressure**.

It usually rains where there is low air pressure.

The weather is usually clear where there is high air pressure.

The sun's rays heat Earth's surface. But some parts of the surface heat up more than other areas. This means that some areas will have low air pressure and others will have high air pressure. Cool air from high-air-pressure areas always moves to replace rising air in low-air-pressure areas. This movement of air is what we call wind. If there is a small difference in air pressure, the wind will be gentle. If there is a big difference, the wind will be strong.

Wind blows due to differences in air pressure.

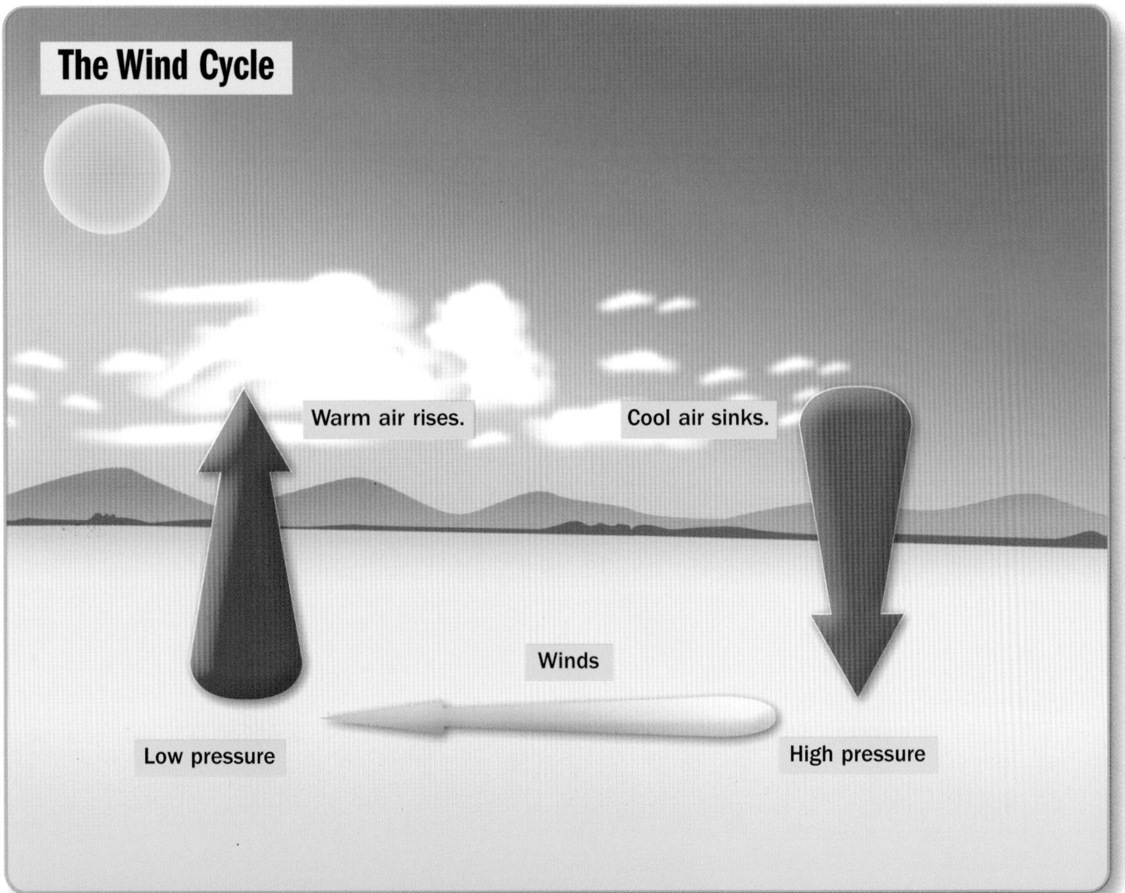

Why Tornadoes Occur

There are two main weather conditions needed for a tornado to form. One is a cold front, and the other is an updraft.

Cold Front The first weather condition needed for a tornado to form is a **front**. When a mass of warm moist air meets a mass of cold dry air, a boundary called a front is formed. A cold front occurs when a mass of cold air is pushed under a warm air mass. This forces the warm air to rise. As the warm air rises, it becomes cooler. As it cools, it forms clouds. Rain usually follows. Tornadoes come from storm clouds that can form along a cold front.

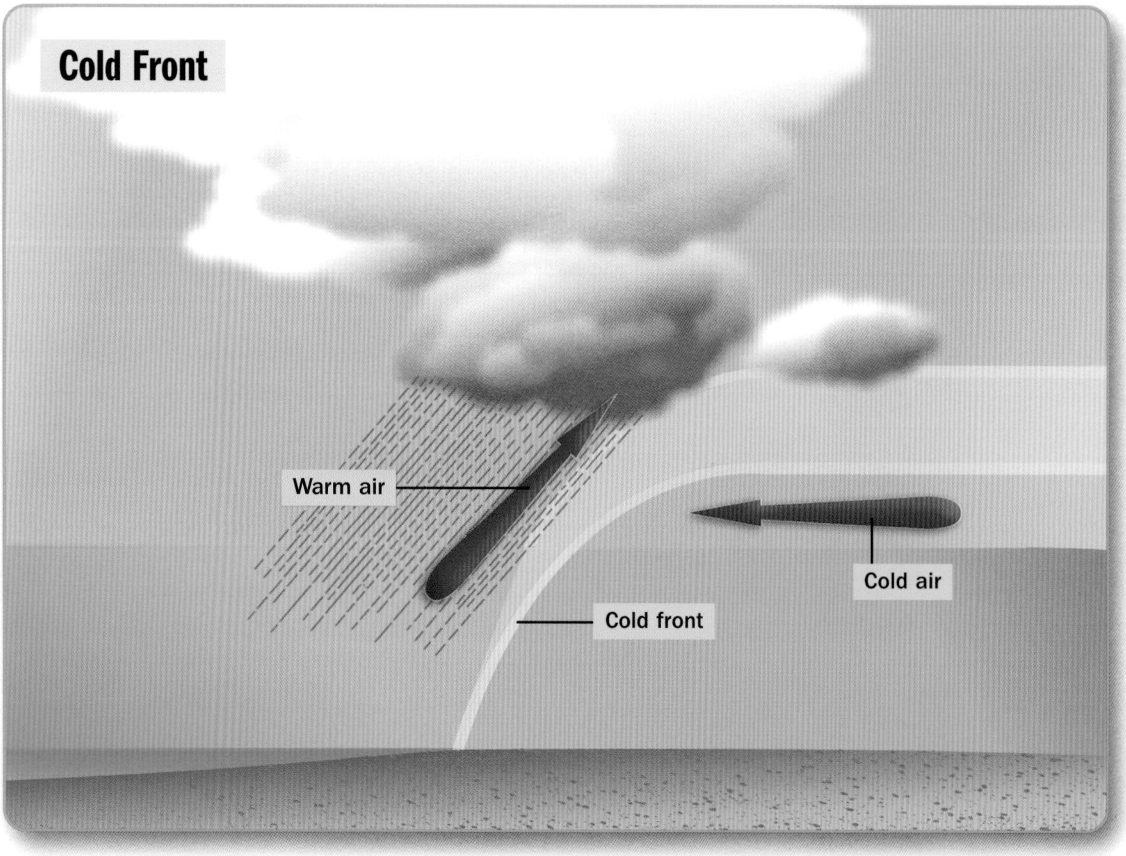

Updraft Tornadoes also need a weather condition called an **updraft** to form. An updraft occurs when warm **humid** air rises quickly from the ground. This happens when the ground gets very hot. The warm humid air passes through a mass of cold air at the bottom of a storm cloud. High winds inside the cloud cause the rising air to spin. The spinning air forms a powerful funnel. The funnel's winds can spin at over 180 kilometers (120 miles) per hour.

The air pressure inside the funnel of air is very low. Because the outside air pressure is a lot higher, and air moves from high-pressure areas to low-pressure areas, outside air is sucked into the updraft.

When the spinning funnel of winds touches land, it becomes a tornado. The eye of the tornado is the low-pressure center of the funnel. The low-pressure center picks up anything in its path.

An updraft causes the strong spinning winds of a tornado.

Key Concept 2 Clouds give meteorologists clues about what is happening in the atmosphere.

Studying the Weather

Meteorologists are people who study weather. One way meteorologists can **forecast**, or predict, the weather is by looking at clouds. They can tell from clouds if the conditions are right for a tornado. Cumulus, cumulonimbus, and wall clouds all give clues about tornado-producing weather.

meteorologists
scientists who study the weather

Cumulus Clouds Cumulus clouds are puffy clouds that look like giant cotton balls. The bases of cumulus clouds are low in the sky. But, because these clouds grow upward rather than across the sky, they can grow quite high.

Cumulus clouds most often appear in clear weather. But, if the right conditions exist, they can grow into violent tornado-producing storm clouds. A towering cumulus is a clue that a storm cloud may form. This cloud looks like a cauliflower because it has a flat base and a lumpy top. It can grow into a giant cumulonimbus.

Cumulus clouds on a fine day

Cumulonimbus Clouds Cumulonimbus clouds produce powerful thunderstorms and, sometimes, tornadoes. Cumulonimbus clouds are the tallest of all clouds—they can reach heights of 18,300 meters (60,000 feet). Their tops often spread out into the shape of an anvil.

The presence of cumulonimbus clouds does not mean that a tornado is on the way. Meteorologists will watch these clouds and look for special signs. One sign that a tornado may develop from a cumulonimbus is when the base of the cloud becomes dark and horizontal with no rain beneath it.

A cumulonimbus with a classic, anvil-shaped top

Wall Clouds A wall cloud hanging down from a rain-free cumulonimbus is a sure sign that the conditions are right for a tornado. A wall cloud hangs down low from the base of the cumulonimbus. It shows the location of a strong updraft. Often wall clouds rotate slowly, forming the shape of a stack of plates. Rotating wall clouds are usually present up to an hour before a tornado forms.

A thick wall cloud sits low in the sky.

Key Concept 3 **Tools and technology help meteorologists gather data about weather.**

Predicting Tornadoes

Meteorologists can predict tornadoes by studying weather conditions. They use special tools and instruments to collect weather **data**, or information. Computers in weather offices use the data to make weather maps. Meteorologists use the weather maps to forecast the weather. If the conditions are right for a tornado, meteorologists can send out warnings. Radar, weather satellites, and weather planes all help meteorologists predict tornadoes.

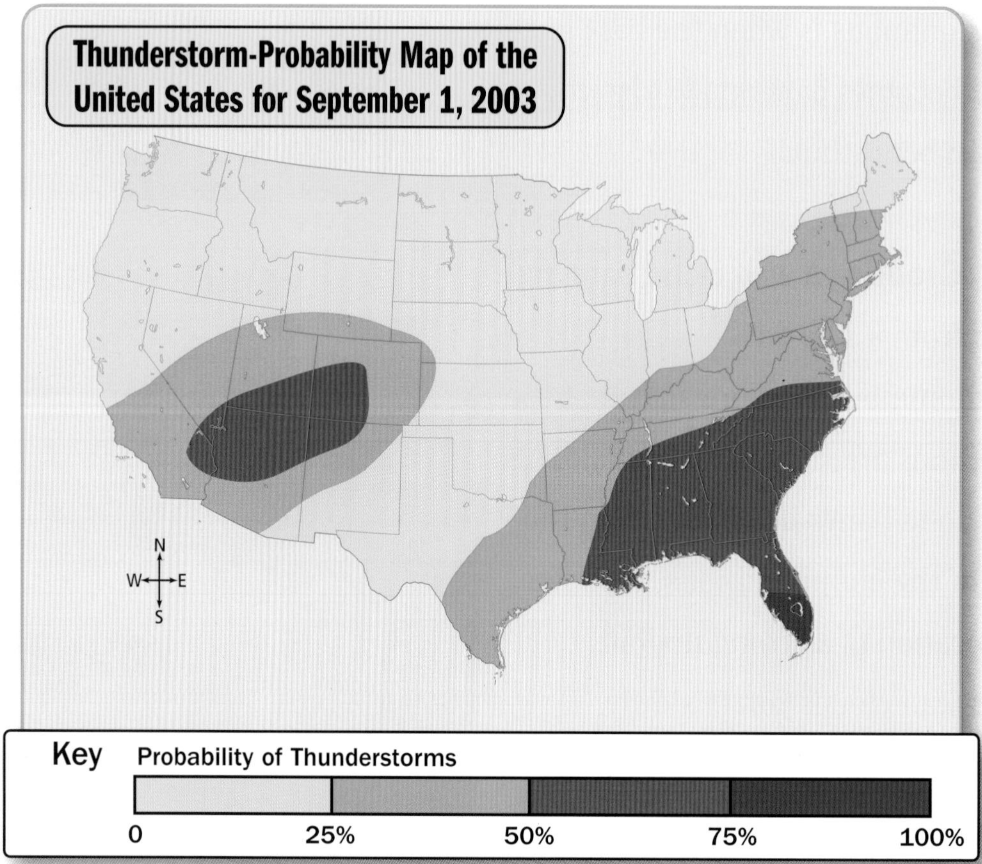

Which part of the country has the highest probability of thunderstorms?

Radar Radar is an important tool used to predict tornadoes. It uses an antenna to send out radio waves. These waves bounce off water in clouds. The waves then return to the antenna. Meteorologists study the returning signals and figure out how much rainfall to expect from a storm.

Radar can detect clouds that might form tornadoes. The computer can sound an alarm when weather patterns are starting to look dangerous. The radar is also used to track a tornado's path once it has begun.

Weather Satellites Weather satellites orbit the Earth in space. Some orbit 35,400 kilometers (22,000 miles) above the Equator. These satellites take photos of clouds and storms and beam them back to Earth. These photos help meteorologists forecast the weather. They can warn people in advance if the weather conditions are right for tornadoes to form.

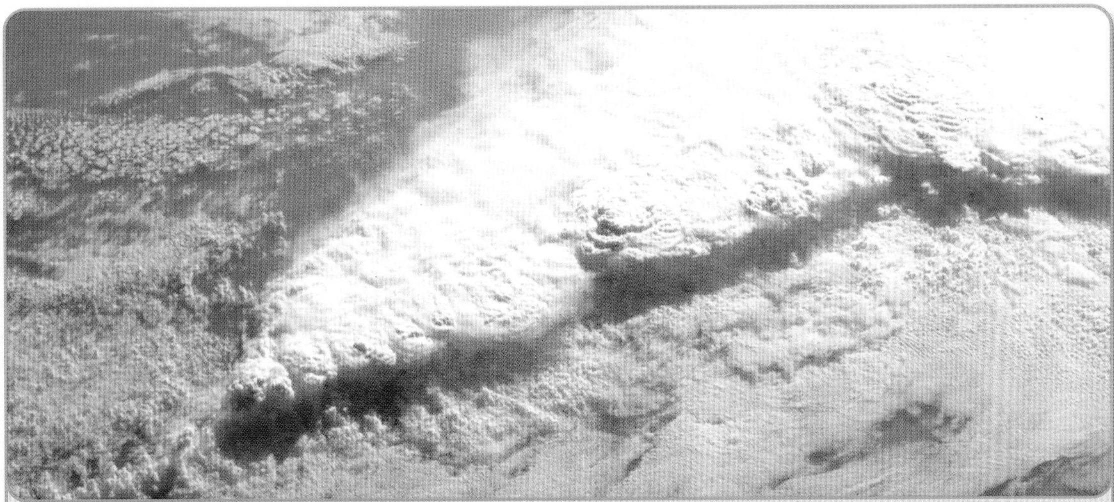

This satellite photo of Florida shows a severe thunderstorm that produced many tornadoes.

Weather Planes Special weather planes travel through storm clouds to collect data on storms that may produce tornadoes. They carry tools under their wings or on their noses. These tools measure temperature, air pressure, and wind speed. Weather stations use the collected data to help predict the weather.

After the Tornado After a tornado, scientists look at the damage to estimate what the tornado's wind speed was. Then, they rate the strength of the tornado on a scale called the **Fujita scale**. The highest rating on the scale is F5. This rating is given to tornadoes that reach speeds of 420–512 kilometers (261–318 miles) per hour.

Damage from a tornado that tore through Tennessee in 2002

Think About the Key Concepts

Think about what you read. Think about the pictures and diagrams. Use these to answer the questions. Share what you think with others.

1. Name one kind of extreme weather. What conditions lead to this weather?

2. What can meteorologists learn about the weather from studying clouds?

3. What tools do meteorologists use to forecast the weather?

4. How does extreme weather affect people and the land?

VISUAL LITERACY

Weather Maps

Weather maps contain information that helps you understand the weather.
Look back at the weather map on page 14. It is a weather map of the United States that shows the forecasted probability of thunderstorms for a certain day.

The weather map on page 19 is a different kind of weather map. It shows the weather conditions that may cause tornadoes in "Tornado Alley." To read a weather map, follow the steps below.

How to Read a Weather Map

1. **Read the title to learn what the map shows.**
   What is this weather map about?
2. **Read the key to learn what the symbols stand for.**
   What do the lines show? What do the letters L and H stand for?
3. **Study the information on the map.**
   In which area might tornadoes occur? What information led you to this conclusion?
4. **Think about what you have learned.**
   If clear weather was likely in a city, would you expect to see a letter H or a letter L near that city on the map?

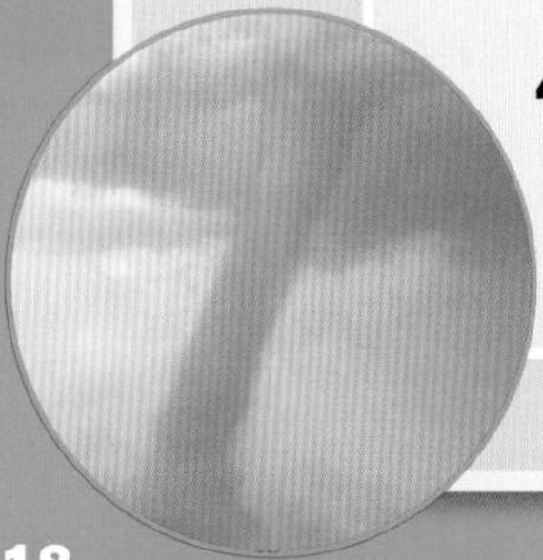

Tornado Conditions in Tornado Alley

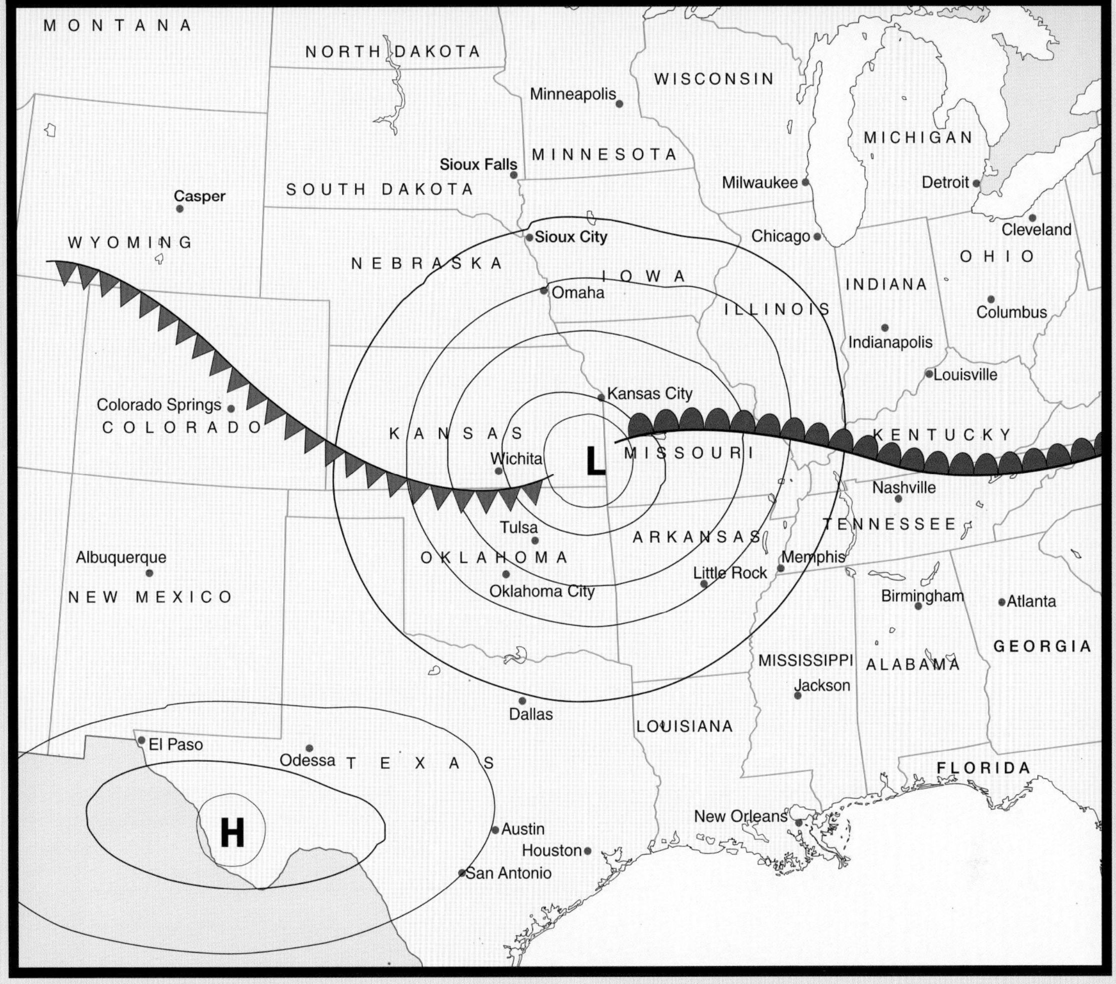

Key

L Area of low air pressure

H Area of high air pressure

Warm front – warm air meets and rises above cold air

Cold front – cold air meets and is pushed under warm air

Isobars – join areas that have the same air pressure

GENRE STUDY

Explanations

An **explanation** can tell how and why something happened. The article starting on page 21 tells about one specific weather event. It explains what happened, why it happened, and what effects it had on the people and land.

An explanation includes the following:

Oklahoma Tornadoes, May 3, 1999

The title tells you the topic.

The introduction tells what the explanation will be about.

Charts, maps, diagrams, and photographs help you picture what you are reading.

The Fujita Scale

Scale	Wind Speed kilometers per hour	miles per hour	Effect
F0	64–116	40–72 mph	Light damage
F1	117–180	73–112	Moderate damage
F2	181–253	113–157	Considerable damage
F3	254–332	158–206	Severe damage
F4	333–419	207–260	Devastating damage
F5	420–512	261–318	Incredible damage

The Introduction

The introduction gives the reader an overview, or the big picture of what the explanation is about.

Body paragraphs give details.

The Tornadoes of May 3, 1999

Body Paragraphs

The body paragraphs make up most of the writing in the explanation. They provide the information and details that help to explain the event.

The conclusion summarizes the text.

The Conclusion

The conclusion summarizes or ties together the information in the explanation.

Oklahoma Tornadoes, May 3, 1999

Tornadoes in the United States usually occur in late spring and summer. On May 3, 1999, central Oklahoma was hit by several very powerful thunderstorms. These storms produced 11 tornadoes that devastated the state.

The **title** tells you the topic.

The **introduction** tells you what the explanation will be about.

One of the tornadoes had the strongest winds ever recorded. It was the tornado that hit the town of Moore, Oklahoma, at 7 o'clock in the evening. Scientists recorded the winds at 512 kilometers (318 miles) per hour. The tornado registered F5 on the Fujita scale.

Maps, diagrams, **charts**, and photographs help you picture what you are reading.

The Fujita Scale

Scale	Wind Speed		Effect
	kilometers per hour	miles per hour	
F0	64–116	40–72	Light damage
F1	117–180	73–112	Moderate damage
F2	181–253	113–157	Considerable damage
F3	254–332	158–206	Severe damage
F4	333–419	207–260	Devastating damage
F5	420–512	261–318	Incredible damage

The Causes of Tornadoes in the Area

Body paragraphs give details.

Oklahoma lies in an area known as "Tornado Alley." The area also includes the states of Iowa, Kansas, Nebraska, and Texas. Tornado Alley is named for the many tornadoes that hit the area.

A supercell thunderstorm in Texas

Most tornadoes occur in Tornado Alley in the spring and early summer. They come from powerful thunderstorms that develop when warm, moist air from the Gulf of Mexico meets cool, dry air from the Rocky Mountains. These thunderstorms are often strong, long-lasting thunderstorms, called supercells. Supercells produce the most powerful and dangerous tornadoes.

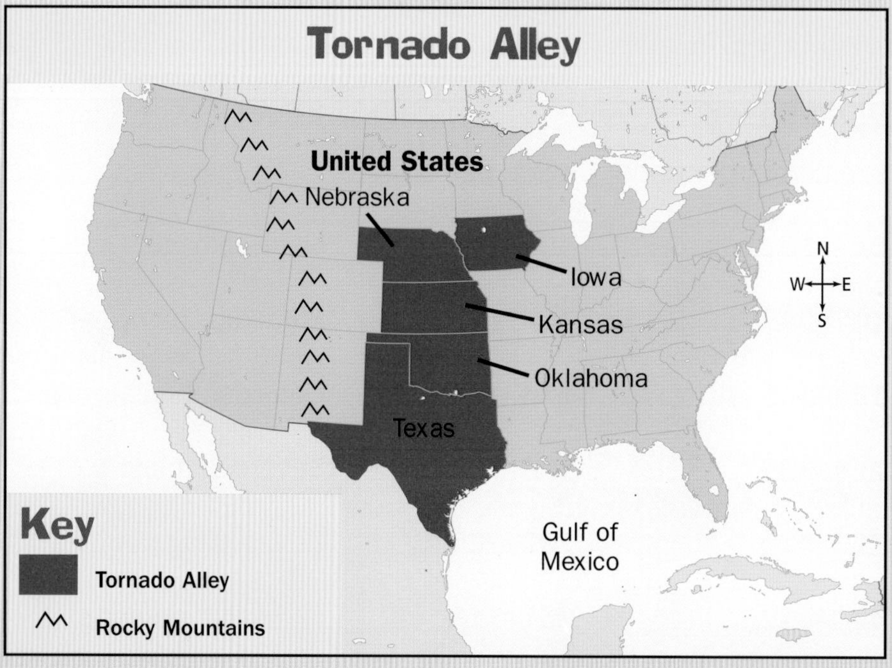

The Tornadoes of May 3, 1999

During the day of May 3, 1999, meteorologists in central Oklahoma noticed weather conditions that can cause thunderstorms. There was a layer of warm, moist air near the ground, and a much cooler layer of air above. These two air masses met and the warm air started to rise. When it stopped rising, it spread out and formed a dark cumulonimbus cloud. The top of this cloud was wide and flat like an anvil.

A jet stream is a current of air high above Earth. This fast-moving wind can often supply energy to a growing storm. In Oklahoma, meteorologists thought that the jet stream would not affect the storm very much because the jet stream winds were not very strong. They thought there would be heavy rain and thunderstorms. But they did not think that these thunderstorms would be powerful enough to allow tornadoes to form.

This photograph of a large cumulonimbus cloud over Oklahoma was taken by a person tracking the storms.

A Supercell Forms

Later in the day, the jet stream increased in speed and fed more energy to the storm. This caused a powerful supercell storm to form near Lawton, Oklahoma. The jet stream winds were now much stronger than the wind closer to the ground. This created a weather condition called wind shear. The rising moist air between the strong jet stream winds and the weaker winds began to spin.

In another area, near Altus, Oklahoma, meteorologists noticed a dryline. A dryline forms in Tornado Alley when cool, dry air from the west collides with warm, moist air from the southeast. If there is enough moisture in the air from the east, severe storms can form along the dryline.

Meteorologists noticed that cumulus clouds were building up near this dryline. A second supercell storm soon formed in the Altus area.

Supercell Thunderstorm

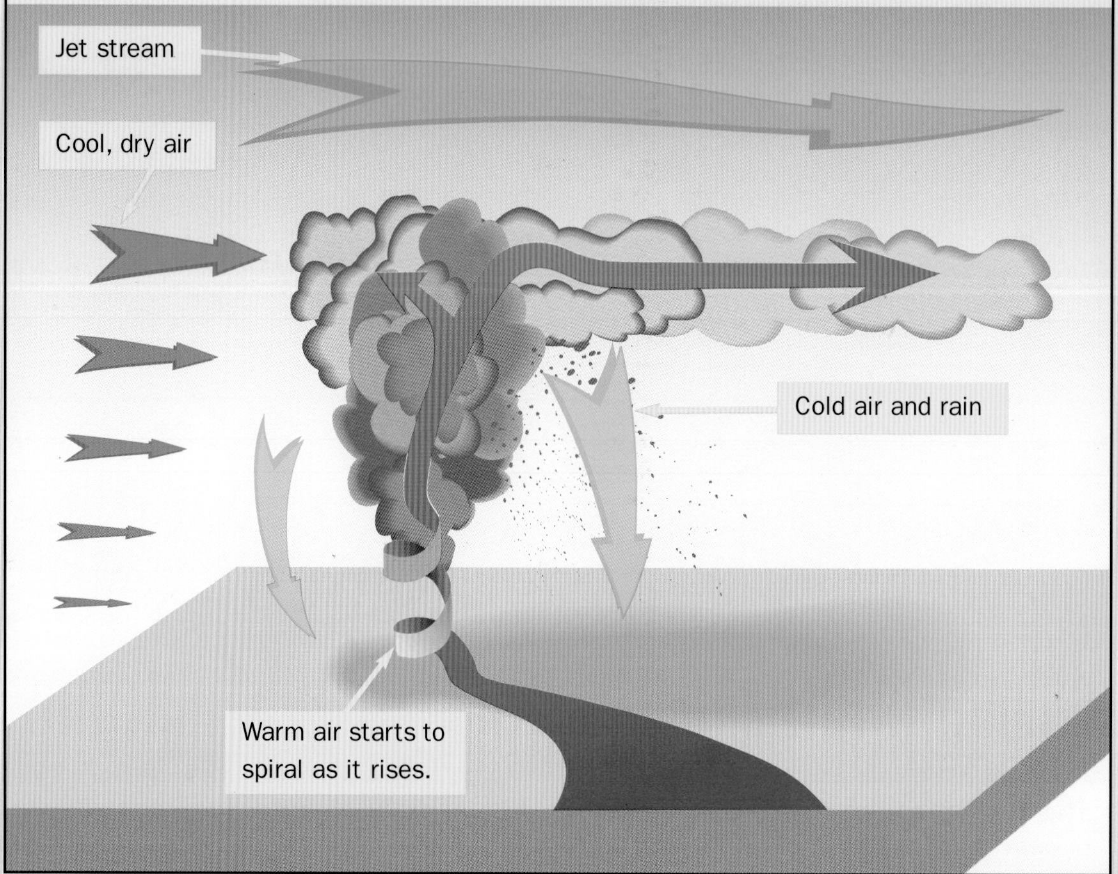

The Storms Worsen

As the storms continued through the day, the horizontal tubes of spinning air in the supercells turned into vertical columns of spinning air. These columns of spinning air, called mesocyclones, usually produce tornadoes.

What had started as low-risk storms quickly changed to high-risk storms. Meteorologists issued a tornado warning in Oklahoma.

By 4 o'clock in the afternoon, the first tornado struck. It was the first of 11 tornadoes to strike the state that day.

Meteorologists tracked the tornadoes using helicopters and radar. Most television stations stayed on the air providing nonstop information. This helped give advance warning to people in the path of the tornadoes.

A mesocyclone tornado hits the ground south of Oklahoma.

The Effects of the Tornadoes

The **conclusion** summarizes the text.

Even though tornadoes do not last long and do not have a wide path when they touch the ground, they can do a lot of damage. The tornadoes of May 3, 1999 killed at least 40 people and injured about 675. The tornadoes destroyed or damaged homes, stores, businesses, churches, and schools. They damaged roads and bridges. They lifted people, trees, and cars into the air. In just a few hours, the tornadoes did more than 1.2 billion dollars worth of damage.

Meteorologists are now working on creating a better warning system to give people more time to prepare for a tornado.

Scientists are also working on providing better protection for people when storms do hit. But one thing scientists cannot do is prevent deadly tornadoes, like the ones that struck Oklahoma in May 1999, from occurring again.

Tornado damage in Oklahoma in May, 1999

Apply the Key Concepts

Key Concept 1 Conditions in the atmosphere, such as air pressure, create weather.

Activity

Research more information about the weather conditions that produce tornadoes. A good place to start is with thunderstorms. Look on the Internet or in books in the library. Make a list to show all the weather conditions that you find.

Key Concept 2 Clouds give meteorologists clues about what is happening in the atmosphere.

Activity

Draw a chart with three columns. In the first column, draw pictures of the different kinds of clouds related to tornadoes. In the second, name each kind of cloud and explain what it looks like. In the third, explain what each cloud tells you about the development of tornadoes. Label your chart "Clouds and Tornadoes."

Key Concept 3 Tools and technology help meteorologists gather data about weather.

Activity

Conduct research to find information about storm chasers. Use the Internet or a library. What sorts of instruments do they use? How do they help predict the path of a tornado? Write a short account of your findings.

RESEARCH AND WRITE

Create Your Own Explanation

There are lots of examples of extreme weather around the world. Some extreme weather may even happen close to where you live. Can you remember a flood or a drought? Can you remember a big storm that turned into a hurricane or caused a tornado?

1. Study the Model

Look back at the description of explanations on page 20. Then, read the article on pages 21–26 again. Look for the examples in the text that tell you this is an explanation. Can you find the opening statement? Can you find the concluding statement? Which paragraphs explain the causes of the weather disaster? Which paragraphs explain the effects of the weather disaster? Look at the diagrams or maps again. Think about how they helped you understand the topic.

2. Choose Your Topic

Now choose one example of an extreme weather event that you would like to find out more about. You may have to start by looking at books on extreme weather, reading newspaper accounts, or using the Internet. Once you've chosen your topic, you're ready to start.

3. Research Your Topic

Ask yourself what you already know about this topic. Do you know enough to write an explanation of how or why it occurred? Probably not. So, you need to make a list of questions that you need to answer. Remember that you are going to write an explanation, so many of your questions may start with "how" or "why." Now go to the library or to the Internet to get your facts.

Monsoon

1. What caused the monsoon?

2. How did the monsoon affect people?

4. Take Notes

Take notes of what you find out. As you find out a new fact, you may find that it leads to another question. Write the new questions down so that you don't forget them. As you write your notes, make a note of the things that you can explain using a diagram or map.

5. Write a Draft

Look back at the facts you found. Do they explain how or why your event occurred? If they do, start writing your draft. You may need to check back with page 20 to remind yourself of the features of an explanation.

6. Revise and Edit

Reread your draft. Does it explain your extreme weather event? Does it have all the features of an explanation? Have you spelled special weather words correctly? Have you drawn charts and maps to help with the explanation?

SHARING YOUR WORK

Present Your Explanation

Now you can share your work. With a group of students, present your explanations as part of a television special report on extreme weather. The program will be called *Explaining Extreme Weather*.

How to Present Your Work

1. **Choose a person in your group to be the anchorperson.**
That person will introduce each member of the group. The anchorperson will also read the opening statement from each explanation.
2. **Collect the equipment you will need.**
Before you make your presentation, you will need to transfer your charts and maps to overhead transparencies or to a piece of poster board.
3. **Rehearse your reading.**
Before you read your explanation you will need to rehearse reading it aloud. Read it aloud several times. Practice looking up at your audience while you are speaking.
4. **When you have finished, be prepared to answer questions.**
Your audience may ask you to explain something in more detail or review some of the facts.
5. **When you have all made your oral presentations, bind the explanations together and make them into a book.**
As a group, make a cover for the book. Then, bind all the pages together with staples or yarn.

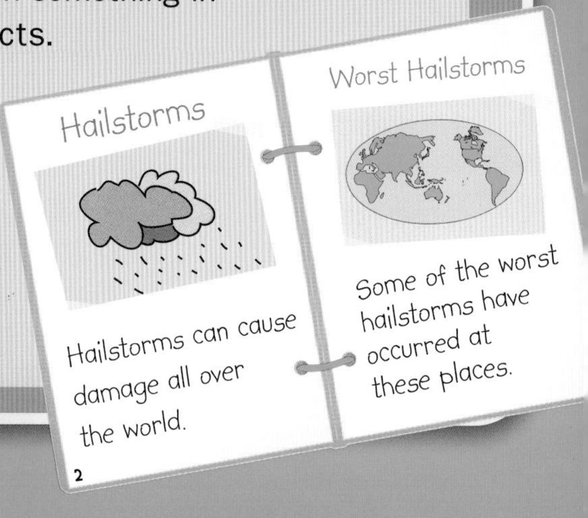

Glossary

air pressure – the effect of air pressing down on Earth's surface

atmosphere – the layer of air that surrounds Earth

data – information that is collected

dense – the result of particles being very close together, making a substance thick or heavy

forecast – to predict what the weather will be like

front – a weather condition that occurs when areas of air with different temperatures meet

Fujita scale – a scale that rates tornadoes according to their wind speed and the damage they cause

high air pressure – a weather condition that occurs when there is a lot of air pressing down on Earth

humid – containing a lot of moisture

low air pressure – a weather condition that occurs when there is not much air pressing down on Earth

meteorologists – scientists who study the weather

particles – very small parts of a substance that cannot be seen with the eye alone

tornado – a spinning funnel of winds that forms in storm clouds and reaches down to land

updraft – the effect of warm, moist air rising quickly

Index

air pressure 8–9, 11, 16

atmosphere 8

cloud 10–13, 15–16

damage 7, 16

eye 11

front 10

Fujita scale 16

meteorologists 12–15

rain 4–5, 10, 13

temperature 8, 16

tornado 4–8, 10–16

Tornado Alley 7

weather 4, 8, 10–12, 14–16

weather offices 14

wind 5–6, 8–9, 11

wind speed 11, 16